Oceans and Seas

Stephen Savage

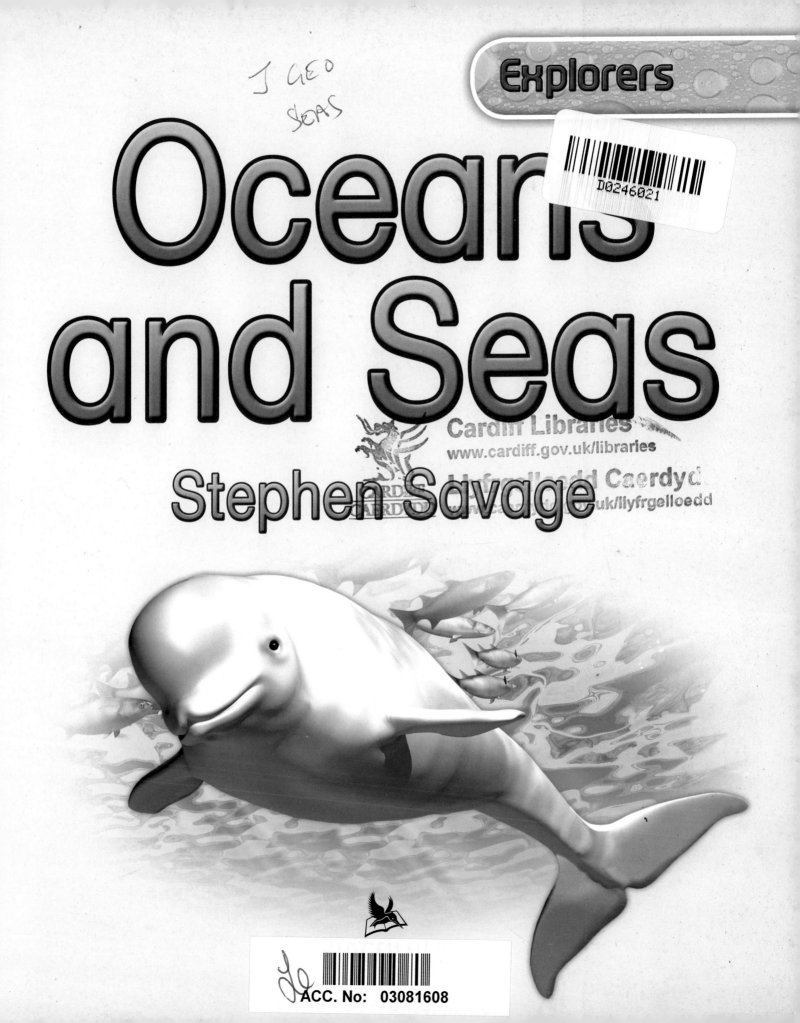

KINGFISHER

First published 2010 by Kingfisher
This edition published 2012 by Kingfisher
an imprint of Macmillan Children's Books
a division of Macmillan Publishers Limited
20 New Wharf Road, London N1 9RR
Basingstoke and Oxford
Associated companies throughout the world
www.panmacmillan.com

Illustrations by: Peter Bull Art Studio

ISBN 978-0-7534-3491-8

Copyright © Macmillan Children's Books 2010

1 3 5 7 9 8 6 4 2
1TR/0512/UNT/WKT/140MA/C

A CIP catalogue record for this book is available from
the British Library.

Printed in China

Picture credits

The Publisher would like to thank the following
for permission to reproduce their material.
(t = top, b = bottom, c = centre, l = left, r = right):
Pages 4l Photolibrary/Sakis Papadopoulos; 5tl Science Photo
Library (SPL)/Planetary Visions; 5tr Nature Picture Library (NPL)/
Georgette Douwma; 5bl Corbis/Karl Weatherly; 5br Alamy/
blickwinkel; 7 Photolibrary/Iain Sarjeant; 8c Photolibrary/
Marevision; 8bl Frank Lane Picture Agency (FLPA)/Yva
Momatiuk & John Eastcott; 9tl Alamy/Premier; 8tr Photolibrary/
Marevision; 8bc FLPA/FotoNatura/FN/Minden; 9br FLPA/Roger
Tidman; 10 Corbis/Stephen Frink/Science Faction; 12cl
Photolibrary/David B Fleetham; 12b NPL/Georgette Douwma;
12-13t Photolibrary/James Watt; 13tr Photolibrary/Roberto
Rinaldi; 13cl Shutterstock; 13cr Corbis/Stuart Westmorland
Science Faction; 13b NPL/Constantinos Petrinos; 14 Corbis/
Norbert Wu/Science Faction; 16c Photolibrary/Reinhard
Dirscherl; 16b Photolibrary/Reinhard Dirscherl; 17tr Corbis/
Jonathan Blair; 17cr Corbis/Adam Woolfitt; 17bl Photolibrary/
David B Fleetham; 17br National Geographic Society/Emory
Kristof; 18 Alamy/Photo Agency EYE; 20tl Corbis/Tim Davis;
20cr Getty Images/Flickr; 21ct Alamy/WaterFrame; 2cr Corbis/
Hal Beral; 21bl Corbis/Paul Souders; 21br FLPA/D P Wilson;
23 NPL/Mark Carwardine; 24tl Photolibrary/Koji Kitagawa;
24cr FLPA/Norbert Wu; 24b NPL/Steven Kazlowski; 25tl NPL/
Jim Watt; 25cr Corbis/Rick Price; 25b Photolibrary/Corbis;
26 NPL/David Shale; 28tl Image Quest Marine/ Carlos Villoch;
29tl SPL/RIA Novosti; 29tr Photolibrary/Paulo De Oliveira;
29cr Image Quest Marine/Peter Batson; 29bl Corbis/Ralph
White; 29br Monterey Bay Aquarium Research Institute,
California; 30cl Shutterstock/Gregor Kervina;
30cr Shutterstock/Juriah Mosin; 30bl Shutterstock/Kuzma;
31tr Shutterstock/Irina Yun; 31cl Shutterstock/Ocean Image
Photography; 31b Shutterstock/Gary Yim

Contents

More to explore

On some of the pages in this book, you will find coloured buttons with symbols on them. There are four different colours, and each belongs to a different topic. Choose a topic, and follow its coloured buttons through the book, and you'll make some interesting discoveries of your own.

For example, on page 6 you'll find a blue button, like this, next to some children investigating rock pools. The blue buttons are about people exploring.

Page 23

People exploring

There is a page number in the button. Turn to that page (page 23) to find a blue button next to something else that people follow and explore. Follow all the steps through the book, and at the end you'll find out how the steps are linked, and discover even more information about this topic.

Animals

Conservation

Science

The other topics in this book are animals, conservation and science. Follow the steps and see what you can discover!

Oceans and seas

The oceans form the largest habitat on Earth, stretching from shallow coastal seas to wide open ocean and down to the dark depths. Seas are part of the oceans. In fact, all the oceans are linked together to form one huge body of water.

This is the Atlantic Ocean, near Lagos, Portugal.

The shallow coastal waters are safe for paddling and swimming.

Coasts are the places where land and sea or ocean meet. They range from beautiful sandy beaches to rugged rocky cliffs. The water here rises and falls twice a day, and this is called a tide.

A wave, formed out in the ocean, is breaking on the beach.

Most sandy beaches are made up of tiny pieces of rock and seashells.

This is the Atlantic Ocean. •••

•••• This is a sea – the Mediterranean Sea.

Around 20,000 species of fish live in the world's oceans.

The Earth is sometimes known as the 'blue planet', because nearly two-thirds of its surface is salt water in the form of oceans and seas. They control our climate and weather and are an important part of the water cycle.

The oceans are precious. Thousands of animal species depend on them, and humans do too. The ocean habitat is easily damaged, so it is important that we look after the oceans and use natural resources more wisely.

fishing boat

People love to live near the sea and enjoy water sports such as surfing, sailing and wind surfing.

At the seashore

The seashore is the place where the land meets the sea. It can be a sandy or pebbly beach, a mudflat or a steep cliff. Much of the seashore is only uncovered at low tide, when rock pools appear and we can take a peek at sea life.

Page 10

Page 23

Page 10

Page 23

① shore crab ② children playing and looking for sea life ③ blenny (a fish) ④ mussels

This is bladder wrack seaweed. Its air pockets help it to float at the surface of the sea.

What is this?

Page 15

As the tide goes out and the sea level drops, many sea creatures stay where they are. Some are stuck onto the rocks and cannot move, while others shelter amongst the rocks that become rock pools. Crabs and prawns are searching for scraps of food, while starfish glide along, feeding on mussels.

 5 prawn

 6 periwinkle, a type of sea snail

7 starfish feeding on mussels

 8 turnstones looking for food

Between the tides

The lives of seashore animals depend on the rise and fall of the tide. At low tide, animals take shelter among the rocks or hide within their sandy burrows. Wading birds come down to the sand to feed.

A scorpion fish hides at the bottom of a rock pool.

seal trapped in a net

Litter floating in the sea can injure and kill wildlife. Animals can swallow litter and choke on it. Many whales, seals, turtles and seabirds become entangled in old fishing nets and drown.

Scorpion fish are often found in rock pools, but are difficult to see because their body pattern matches the surroundings. They lie in wait, ready to gulp down any prawn or small fish that comes too close.

This unlucky prawn is about to become a meal for the scorpion fish!

Hermit crabs do not grow their own shells like other crabs do. Instead they live inside empty seashells to protect the soft part of their body. As the crab grows it must find a bigger shell.

A cockle has feeding tubes which it uses to eat tiny creatures.

Wading birds feed on sandy shores and muddy estuaries at low tide. Each species has a special type of beak suitable for reaching the shellfish and worms that live at different depths beneath the sand.

The oystercatcher can eat worms and open mussel shells.

The ringed plover has a short beak to catch animals just beneath the surface.

A coral landscape

A coral reef is like a colourful underwater city, built by millions of tiny animals called coral polyps. Hundreds of different types of fish and invertebrates (animals without backbones) find food and shelter in the coral reef too, and it is bursting with colour and life.

Page 19

What is this?

This is a close-up view of the knobbly coral skeleton of staghorn coral.

Page 26

The coral polyps are the quiet heart of this lively scene. These tiny animals grow stony skeletons that protect their soft bodies. They live on the surface of their skeletons and catch food with stinging tentacles. All the coral skeletons make a huge reef, where hundreds of fish swim and feed. Larger animals such as sharks may visit, too.

 staghorn coral, a common reef-building coral

 brain coral looks like a human brain

6 clown fish swimming safely within the tentacles of an anemone

Life on the reef

The reef is home to a surprising variety of animals. It provides them with food and shelter. Some reef fish hunt among the corals, while others find food in more unusual ways.

manta ray

cleaner wrasse

Manta rays swim gracefully through the water by flapping their large wing-like fins. They are the largest of all the rays and can measure five metres from wing tip to wing tip. These fish are harmless to humans, and feed on plankton.

Cleaner wrasse set up cleaning stations where they gobble up flea-like creatures that live on other fish. The wrasse performs a dance to attract a 'customer', who may even allow the wrasse to clean inside its mouth.

This colourful fish has a mouth like a parrot's beak.

Parrotfish use their strong beak-like teeth to feed on algae and coral polyps. Any coral skeleton that they swallow is ground up by teeth in their throat. Some sand around coral reefs is actually parrotfish poo.

These large fleshy horns guide water and plankton into the ray's mouth ••••

Lionfish are brightly coloured as a warning: they're poisonous!

Healthy coral reefs are brightly coloured and full of life. Special algae living inside the coral polyps provide extra food needed by the coral to build their stony skeletons.

Algae (the green spots) live in the coral.

This coral is white, or bleached, because the algae that lived in its polyps has died. ••••

Coral is damaged when seas get hotter due to global warming. Higher temperatures kill the algae. Without the extra food from the algae, the coral polyps die and other marine life disappears.

Page 27

1 longfin bannerfish

2 underwater camera

3 People dive in pairs for safety.

What is this?

Exploring a wreck

Lying hidden on the world's seabeds are many shipwrecks – the sad remains of journeys that ended in disaster. Diving to explore these shipwrecks is a fascinating chance to discover hidden history or experience marine life up close.

6

Page 22

4

5

Divers explore a shipwreck and discover that this man-made object has become part of the ocean world, home to many different animals. They find sponges and corals growing on the deck, and watch schools of brightly coloured fish dart to shelter inside the ship. They also meet moray eels and barracuda, lurking and looking for a meal.

This is a close-up view of a sea urchin's spines, which protect it from predators.

Stories under the sea

Every shipwreck has a story to tell. Many sank in storms, while others were the result of sea battles. The objects found on board and the ships themselves provide valuable information about life in the past as well as clues to how the ships sank.

The mast on this ship can still be seen, and there may be plenty for archaeologists to investigate inside the wreck.

soft coral growing on the wreck

A marine archaeologist
is a historian who studies human history underwater – shipwrecks! This one is carefully exploring a shipwreck full of glass bottles and jars that sank in the 11th century.

A shipwreck
in a tropical ocean may become a miniature reef. These wrecks make exciting sites for divers to explore as almost every surface is covered in marine life.

These objects will be displayed in a museum.

coins from the Tudor shipwreck the Mary Rose

Bluestripe snappers cruise around a wreck.

The Titanic sank in 1912, and 1,517 people died. In 1985, the explorer Robert Ballard discovered this famous shipwreck at over 3,900m deep.

What is this?

1 gannet diving to catch fish

2 dolphin swimming quickly towards the school

3 copper shark

1

Page 30

3

2

Feeding time

In the open ocean there is nowhere to hide, and many small fish live in big groups called schools. A school is an easy target for attack, but gives each fish a better chance of surviving. Sharks, dolphins, seals and diving birds attack all at the same time.

4 | dolphin bursting through the bait ball

5 | sardines on the edge of the huge school

6 | Cape fur seal catching a fish

5

4

Page 23

In summertime, enormous schools of sardines travel along Africa's eastern coast, feeding on plankton. These sardines are swimming as a swirling mass of silvery fish called a bait ball. Many predators are attracted to this bait ball. They avoid each other and instead concentrate on catching the fish.

6

This is a close-up view of some sardines – there may be hundreds of thousands in a bait ball.

Oceans full of food

Ocean animals have developed many different ways to find and eat a meal. There are fast and fearsome hunters and slow, gentle plant-eaters. There are masters of camouflage that can creep up unseen and whales that scoop up a huge mouthful of ocean.

Dolphins use their powerful tail to swim fast, and their flippers for steering.

Green sea turtles feed on sea grasses and algae.

Dolphins are meat-eaters.

Green turtles dive for up to five minutes to feed.

Dolphins often work together to catch their prey, for example when they chase a sardine bait ball. They swim fast and catch fish and squid using their sharp pointed teeth. They swallow their food whole.

A cuttlefish is a meat-eater.

The cuttlefish has suckers on its eight arms to hold onto the food it catches.

A cuttlefish catches prey by shooting out two long tentacles. It has a strong beak that can even bite through a crab's tough shell. When attacked, a cuttlefish can squirt out ink as a defence.

A humpback whale eats tiny plankton.

Leafy sea dragons are camouflaged to look like floating seaweed. They drift through the seaweed hunting small fish and shrimps.

Sea dragons eat tiny plankton.

Many ocean animals feed on tiny plant and animal plankton.

Huge **humpback whales** feed on tiny plankton, too. Instead of teeth, they have bristly baleen plates, which they use to sieve tiny foods from the water.

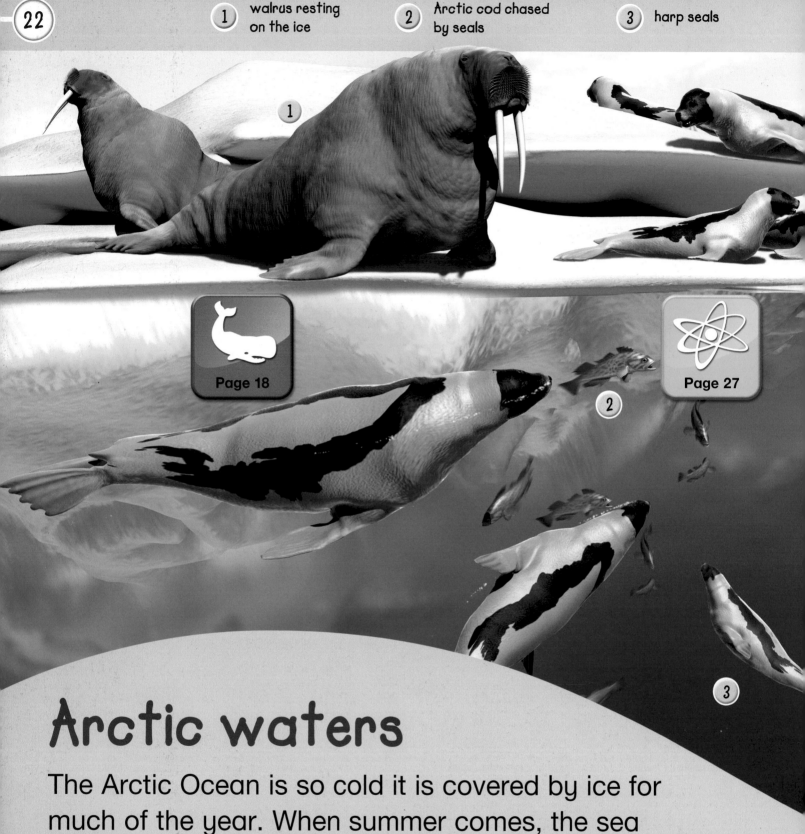

1. walrus resting on the ice
2. Arctic cod chased by seals
3. harp seals

Page 18

Page 27

Arctic waters

The Arctic Ocean is so cold it is covered by ice for much of the year. When summer comes, the sea ice begins to melt and the Arctic bursts into life. Many birds and mammals, both large and small, travel north to these rich feeding grounds.

4 Arctic terns visit the Arctic each summer.

5 Beluga whale calves are born grey.

6 humpback whale

What is this?

Page 30

Page 14

4

6

A pod, or group, of beluga whales glides through the icy water. These white whales spend all year in the Arctic. The seals and walruses are here all year round, too. They feed under water but rest on land. All these mammals have a thick layer of fatty blubber under their skin to keep them warm.

5

This is a close-up view of a walrus's whiskers. Like all mammals, the walrus has hair.

Polar seas

In summer, the Arctic has sunlight for 24 hours a day. Sunlight allows large amounts of plankton to grow, providing food for the animals that live there and attracting summer visitors. When it is summer in the Antarctic, the same happens there.

Seals are born on land. Newborn harp seal pups have a white fur coat. This snowy camouflage helps protect them against predators such as polar bears.

The lion's mane jellyfish is the longest animal, with tentacles 30m long.

Polar bears spend much of their time on the sea ice hunting seals. They can also swim for hours at a time using their large, powerful front paws as paddles.

This humpback whale calf was born in the winter in the warm, calm seas near Hawaii.

This large sea spider lives on the Antarctic sea floor.

Adult humpback whales eat over 1,000kg of tiny animals a day.

The **Antarctic** is home to thousands of penguins. These birds dive into the water to catch shrimps and fish.

Humpback whales visit the Arctic each summer to feed. They build up fat, which they then live off for about eight months while they travel back to warmer seas for the winter.

Adélie penguins live on the Antarctic ice.

Penguins cannot fly, but are excellent swimmers.

Voyage to the deep

Far beneath the surface of the ocean where the sunlight cannot reach, there lurk many strange and unusual animals. It is much too far down for a human to swim, but people can explore these depths from a manned submersible.

Page 22

What is this?

1 gulper eel with a huge mouth for scooping

2 fangfish with big, sharp fangs (teeth)

3 deep-sea squid

? This is a close-up photo of an anglerfish's lure. This attracts fish into its mouth.

27

A submersible travels into a world of fearsome-looking animals. They are attracted by the submersible's searchlights. Scary-looking fish with needle-sharp teeth and a gulper eel with a giant mouth swim by. Strange creatures that make their own light in the darkness drift past.

Page 30

Page 30

4

5

6

4 Deep-sea jellyfish use tentacles to catch prey.

5 The submersible glides through the water.

6 deep-sea anglerfish

minisub equipped for underwater exploration

The pilot and two others squeeze into the small cabin.

The minisub protects the divers from pressure and the cold. Outside the submersible the weight of the seawater above would crush a human. The water temperature is a near-freezing 3–4°C.

Deep-sea exploration

The deep ocean is the last truly undiscovered place on Earth. More people have been to the Moon than the deep ocean. About 99 per cent of it is still unexplored, and there are many new discoveries still to be made.

Mir is a Russian submersible that has explored the deep-sea regions of the Antarctic and Arctic. Here it is being launched from a ship.

The Mir life-support system can support three people for three days.

Life on the ocean floor is examined from the Mir submersible. Mir can take movie footage and photographs and collect specimens with a mechanical arm. It can reach depths of 6,000m.

Ratfish eat up the remains of sea creatures that have died and sunk to the ocean floor.

Lantern fish are covered in little spots of light, which may attract their prey. They produce it with a chemical reaction like the one that lights up glow sticks.

The dumbo octopus has fins a bit like elephants' ears.

The **sea pig** is a type of sea cucumber that travels across the deep sea floor, hoovering up tiny particles of food in the mud.

deep-sea
anglerfish

The blue-ringed **octopus** is one of the world's most poisonous animals. Octopuses have large brains for their size, and are very intelligent.

The deep-sea anglerfish is just one of 20,000 species of **fish** to be found in the world's oceans. All types of fish have a backbone, scales, fins and gills.

Animals

Science

The **Moon** is the driving force behind tides. Its gravity pulls at the world's oceans, making them rise and fall as the Moon circles the Earth.

An **aqua lung** is a piece of equipment that allows people to breathe under water. It consists of a high-pressure cylinder of air or a special mix of diving gases.

People exploring

A **rock pool** is a brilliant place to start exploring the oceans. Count different types of seaweed and shells, and see if you can spot crabs, prawns, fish and starfish.

Whale-watching expeditions allow scientists to keep track of where whales go each year, and learn about individual animals and their behaviour. Tourists can often join in, too.

humpback
whale

Conservation

Beaches need to be kept free of **rubbish**, which is a disaster for wildlife. Animals can choke on or get trapped by plastic. Pollution kills animals and plants.

Coral reefs around the world are in danger. Pollution destroys many reef creatures. Warming waters cause coral to lose the algae they need to survive.

More to explore

harp seals in the Arctic Ocean

The **harp seal** is a marine mammal, like whales, dolphins and walruses. It can stay underwater for a long time, but comes to the surface to breathe air and also spends time on land.

They may not live in the water, but many kinds of **birds** depend on the oceans for their food. This gannet dives deep into the water to catch fish.

Arctic animals are brilliantly adapted to survive the cold. Fish that live in polar seas produce a special anti-freeze that stops ice crystals from forming in their bodies. This stops them from freezing solid.

Arctic cod

Some animals that live in the deepest, darkest parts of the oceans are **bioluminescent**. This means they glow in the dark. Chemicals in their bodies allow them to do this.

Underwater archaeologists study shipwrecks and other evidence of human history in the oceans. They may examine objects on the sea floor or carefully bring them to the surface.

A **deep-sea submersible** allows scientists to travel to the furthest depths of the ocean – as deep as 6,000m! There they can take photographs and coll samples to study.

deep-sea submersible

Many **dolphins** are protected species, which means it is against the law to harm them. Even so, many are hurt accidentally by fishing nets.

diven
diving
dolphins
Earth 5

More to explore

harp seals in the
Arctic Ocean

The **harp seal** is a marine mammal, like whales, dolphins and walruses. It can stay underwater for a long time, but comes to the surface to breathe air and also spends time on land.

They may not live in the water, but many kinds of **birds** depend on the oceans for their food. This gannet dives deep into the water to catch fish.

Arctic animals are brilliantly adapted to survive the cold. Fish that live in polar seas produce a special anti-freeze that stops ice crystals from forming in their bodies. This stops them from freezing solid.

Arctic cod

Some animals that live in the deepest, darkest parts of the oceans are **bioluminescent**. This means they glow in the dark. Chemicals in their bodies allow them to do this.

Underwater archaeologists study shipwrecks and other evidence of human history in the oceans. They may examine objects on the sea floor or carefully bring them to the surface.

A **deep-sea submersible** allows scientists to travel to the furthest depths of the ocean – as deep as 6,000m! There they can take photographs and collect samples to study.

deep-sea submersible

Many **dolphins** are protected species, which means it is against the law to harm them. Even so, many are hurt accidentally by fishing nets.

Global warming is causing the ice sheets at the poles to melt. This makes life even harder for polar animals, and will cause sea levels to rise around the world.

Index